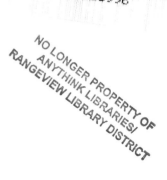

D0620996

21st Century Skills INNOVATION *Library*

From Birds to . . . Aircraft

by Josh Gregory

INNOVATIONS FROM   NATURE

CHERRY LAKE
Publishing

Published in the United States of America by Cherry Lake Publishing
Ann Arbor, Michigan
www.cherrylakepublishing.com

Content Adviser: Jacob Zeiger, Aeronautical Engineer, the Boeing Company, Seattle, Washington

Design: The Design Lab

Photo Credits: Cover and page 3, ©ssuaphotos/Shutterstock, Inc.; cover inset, ©Victor Tyakht/
Shutterstock, Inc.; page 4, ©Georgios Kollidas/Shutterstock, Inc.; page 6, ©Steve Bower/
Shutterstock, Inc.; page 7, ©Mary Evans Picture Library/Alamy; page 9, ©Sergey Uryadnikov/
Dreamstime.com; page 10, ©Atlaspix/Shutterstock, Inc.; page 13, ©INTERFOTO/Alamy; page 15,
©Pictorial Press Ltd/Alamy; page 16, ©MARKA/Alamy; page 20, ©Everett Collection Inc/Alamy;
page 21, ©1971yes/Shutterstock, Inc.; page 23, ©Shutter Lover/Shutterstock, Inc.; page 25,
©Everett Collection Inc/Alamy; page 27, ©ASSOCIATED PRESS; page 28, ©World History
Archive/Alamy.

Library of Congress Cataloging-in-Publication Data
Gregory, Josh.
 From birds to aircraft/by Josh Gregory.
    p. cm.–(Nature's inventors)
 Includes bibliographical references and index.
 ISBN 978-1-61080-497-4 (lib. bdg.) – ISBN 978-1-61080-584-1 (e-book) –
ISBN 978-1-61080-671-8 (pbk.)
 1. Aeronautics–Juvenile literature. 2. Airplanes–Juvenile literature. 3. Birds–Flight–Juvenile
literature. I. Title.
TL547.G865 2012
629.13–dc23   2012001735

Cherry Lake Publishing would like to acknowledge
the work of The Partnership for 21st Century Skills.
Please visit www.21stcenturyskills.org for more information.

Printed in the United States of America
Corporate Graphics Inc.
January 2012
CLFA11

CONTENTS

Chapter One
Up in the Air   4

Chapter Two
First in Flight   9

Chapter Three
The First Airplanes   15

Chapter Four
Flying into the Future   20

Chapter Five
Famous Flyers   25

Glossary   30
For More Information   31
Index   32
About the Author   32

CHAPTER ONE

Up in the Air

Leonardo da Vinci was one of many inventors to experiment with flying machines.

Have you ever seen a bird soaring through the sky and wondered what it would be like to have wings of your own? People have long been amazed and inspired by these incredible animals. Even hundreds of years ago, people were searching for ways to join birds up in the air.

In 1507, Italian inventor John Damian de Falcuis was living in Scotland, working for King James IV. Damian hoped to impress the king by building his own set of wings and learning to fly. He used chicken feathers to construct the wings and strapped them to his arms. He then jumped from the castle walls, planning to fly south toward France. Instead, he fell to the ground and broke his leg. Damian blamed his failure to fly on the chicken feathers, but the problem was actually much more complicated.

Around the same time, fellow inventor Leonardo da Vinci was conducting his own studies of flight back in Italy. During the late 1400s and early 1500s, da Vinci watched birds closely as they flew. He wrote down his observations in a book called *Codex on the Flight of Birds*. He also sketched plans for many different flying machines based on his observations. He built and tested several of the machines, but none was able to fly.

Long before Damian and da Vinci, people in China, Indonesia, and other Eastern countries found success in the skies with kites. The first kites were built several thousand years ago. They were made from cloth and wood. They were often shaped like birds or simple rectangles. Many were used for religious ceremonies. Later, some civilizations built giant kites that could be attached to people. The people could ride the huge kites up into the sky and attack or spy on their enemies. However, kites were not true flying machines. They always needed to be attached to the ground with ropes.

Thousands of years passed before humans successfully built aircraft that did not have to be attached to the ground. These early aircraft were not the airplanes and helicopters we use most often today. They were hot air balloons. The hot air balloon was invented by the French brothers Joseph-Michel and

Today's hot air balloons are made in a wide variety of bright colors and patterns.

The Montgolfier brothers amazed crowds with their first balloon flights.

Jacques-Étienne Montgolfier. They discovered that a paper or cloth bag could be used to collect hot air from a heat source, such as a fire, located below it. The light, hot air causes the bag to rise.

On September 19, 1783, the Montgolfiers sent a sheep, a duck, and a rooster into the sky aboard their

Learning & Innovation Skills

 Leonardo da Vinci was more than just an inventor with an interest in flying machines. He was also a highly successful painter, sculptor, and architect. He is perhaps most famous for his paintings *Mona Lisa* and *Last Supper*. Da Vinci devoted his life to learning as much as he could about the world. He kept detailed notebooks filled with drawings and observations about a wide range of subjects. Today, he is remembered as one of the most brilliant artists and scientists of his time.

balloon. On November 21, they repeated the flight with human test pilots. It was the first time humans had ever flown in a device that was not attached to the ground. The Montgolfiers' discovery eventually led to the creation of other aircraft such as the blimp and the zeppelin. These aircraft use gas-filled balloons to lift passengers and cargo into the air. Like the heated air in hot air balloons, the gases within the containers are lighter than the air outside. This causes the aircraft to float upward.

Today, thousands of airplanes fly every day. We use them to travel across entire continents in just hours. Airplanes carry people and goods to destinations all around the world. Planes are even used in war. But how did humans learn to use their observations of birds to build such incredible flying machines? Kites, balloons, and the experiments of early thinkers such as da Vinci were just part of the journey into flight. The hard work and amazing discoveries of many other inventors would make air travel what it is today.

CHAPTER TWO

First in Flight

John Damian believed that humans could fly just as birds do. However, it is impossible for people to fly by simply flapping a pair of wings. A person's muscles aren't strong enough. Early inventors such as Damian failed to realize just how powerful a bird's chest muscles must be to fly.

Whether they are birds, airplanes, or hot air balloons, all objects in flight must contend with four different

Birds use strong chest muscles to flap their wings.

Birds use momentum to glide through the sky without flapping their wings.

forces. Thrust is forward force. It pushes an object from behind. Lift is upward force. It pushes the object from below. Drag is resistance from the air the object is moving through. It pushes the object from the front. Finally, weight is the force of gravity pulling the object toward the earth.

Birds can generate thrust and lift at the same time by flapping their wings at an angle. This pushes air both below and behind them. Because airplane wings cannot flap as bird wings can, airplanes cannot generate thrust in the same way. They generate thrust by using propellers or **jet** engines. These devices push air behind the airplane, causing it to move forward.

Have you ever seen a bird glide without flapping its wings? Once it has built up speed by flapping, it is able to coast on its forward **momentum**. By keeping its wings stretched out, it can continue to generate lift without generating additional thrust. But how exactly does this work?

In 1738, Swiss scientist Daniel Bernoulli discovered that fast-moving fluids produce less **pressure** than slow-moving ones. The same is true of air. It is this principle that allows birds to glide through the air without flapping their wings. Birds' wings are curved on top but flat on the bottom. Air moves more quickly over

Learning & Innovation Skills

Around the same time George Cayley was conducting his research, British inventor William Henson was exploring his own ideas for aircraft. In 1843, he patented an idea for a device he called the aerial steam carriage. Henson's design was based on the idea of attaching a steam engine to a glider. Though the invention was never actually built, it was one of the earliest suggestions for a powered aircraft.

the curved tops of the wings than it does underneath. As a result, the pressure pressing on the wings from below is greater than the pressure pushing from above. This lifts the birds into the air.

Airplanes work in much the same way. Thrust provided by the propeller or jet pushes the plane forward. The plane gains speed until it is moving fast enough to change the pressure above and below the wings. The plane then lifts into the air. This is why airplanes take off from long runways.

Several people contributed to these discoveries over several decades. Their earliest successes were not with powered airplanes, however. They instead built gliders, which lacked the propellers or jets that airplanes use to generate thrust. As a result, gliders could only fly from high ground to lower ground.

A British scientist named George Cayley built the first successful glider. In 1849, he designed a glider that was able to carry a young boy as its pilot for a short distance. Four years later, he had improved his design

Some of George Cayley's designs looked very different from today's aircraft.

enough that it could support the weight of a grown person. Cayley wrote about his experiments in a book called *On Aerial Navigation*. In it, he became the first to notice that curved surfaces can generate stronger lift than flat ones can. He also suggested using multiple sets of wings to create even more lift.

German **engineer** Otto Lilienthal was born in 1848. As a teenager, he and his brother were fascinated by the aircraft experiments of inventors such as George Cayley. They began building experimental gliders of their own. Lilienthal continued to study the science of flight as he grew older. He knew that birds were the key to solving the mysteries of aircraft construction, and he observed them very carefully. In 1889, he published a book titled *Birdflight as the Basis of* **Aviation**. The book contained observations about the shapes of bird wings and outlined the basic principles of how curved surfaces can be used to generate lift.

Lilienthal built his first successful glider in 1891. Unlike earlier gliders, the pilot could control its direction by shifting his weight. Lilienthal went on to build 18 different glider models. Some were successful, and others were not. Some of his designs had flapping wings. Like previous aircraft built around flapping wings, they were unable to fly. Lilienthal had gone on more than 2,000 flights by 1896, when he was killed in a glider crash. While his death was tragic, it inspired two brothers from Ohio to continue his legacy. Their work would change the world forever.

CHAPTER THREE

The First Airplanes

In 1892, Wilbur and Orville Wright opened up a bicycle shop in their hometown of Dayton, Ohio. They soon became known for their ability to customize bikes just how customers wanted them. The store was a success, and it gave the Wright brothers the money they needed to begin their next project.

The brothers were inspired by the experiments of Otto Lilienthal. Around

The Wright brothers made incredible advances in flying technology.

the time of Lilienthal's death in 1896, they began researching to build experimental aircraft of their own. This led them to develop several new methods of controlling a glider in midair. The brothers came up with the idea of adding a winglike device called an **elevator** to the front of the glider. By changing the elevator's angle, the pilot could control the amount of lift that was

The Wright brothers used levers and pulleys to control their gliders.

applied to the nose of the aircraft. This changed the aircraft's **pitch** by pointing the nose up or down. The Wrights also designed a flexible **rudder** for the back of their glider. By changing its angle, the pilot could turn the aircraft toward the left or the right. This type of motion is known as an aircraft's yaw.

The brothers also created a way to control the glider's **roll**. Previous inventors had often assumed that aircraft had to be stable. Much like a vehicle on the ground, scientists thought an aircraft should stay horizontal as much as possible. The Wrights' experience with bicycles led them to believe that aircraft should also tip sideways. Like a person on a bicycle leaning to the side as he makes a turn, an aircraft could roll to perform tight turns or even complete rotations, called barrel rolls. The Wrights learned that twisting the angle of one of the glider's wings would cause it to lift higher than the other wing and produce roll. Movable flaps called **ailerons** were later added to the backs of airplane wings to create this movement.

Life & Career Skills

Orville and Wilbur Wright were incredibly dedicated to building a working airplane. They thought of little else while conducting their experiments and building new gliders. When they first arrived at their test site near Kitty Hawk, North Carolina, in 1900, they spent their nights sleeping in a tent. It was not until 1902 that they finally built beds and a small kitchen in the wooden shed they used as a workshop.

The Wright brothers used information from Lilienthal's experiments to determine how long and wide the glider's wings needed to be. The wings, elevator, and tail rudder were attached to wires. The glider was designed so that a pilot could lie on his belly and use his hands to tilt the elevator while his hips controlled the wings and the tail rudder.

In October 1900, the brothers were ready to test their invention. They found the perfect test site just outside the town of Kitty Hawk, North Carolina. It was a windy area with plenty of hills from which a glider could take off. For the first test, the Wrights attached a rope to the glider and flew it like a kite. It worked, but not as well as the brothers had hoped. They continued to test the glider over the next couple of years, sometimes with a pilot, and made tweaks to improve it. They increased the size of the glider's wings and altered their shapes. The brothers also adjusted the glider's controls. By 1902, they had mastered control of the glider. They piloted their glider on hundreds of flights that year. It was time to move on to a new challenge.

In 1903, the Wright brothers began experimenting with engines. They asked several engine manufacturers to build them a lightweight, powerful engine, but none of the companies would agree to make what the Wrights needed. Instead, the brothers decided to build it themselves, with the help of their shop mechanic, Charlie Taylor. It took them just six weeks to build a motor that was both lighter and more powerful than they had originally hoped. They also began researching propeller shapes to find one that would provide the thrust needed to power their new aircraft.

By December 1903, they had finished building the world's first true airplane. On December 14, they prepared for its first test flight. Wilbur was the pilot. He started the engine and the plane began moving forward. It lifted off the ground after traveling about 35 feet (10.7 meters). However, Wilbur tried to lift the plane too quickly, and it fell to the ground after three and a half seconds. Wilbur was not hurt, but the airplane was damaged.

Three days later, the brothers had completed repairs and were ready to try again. They were much more successful this time. Orville climbed into the airplane and took off. He kept the plane in the air for about 12 seconds, traveling 120 feet (36.6 m) before landing. It was the first successful airplane flight in history. The Wrights performed three more flights that day, taking turns at the controls. On the last one, Wilbur flew 852 feet (259.7 m) in 59 seconds. Five local people watched in amazement as the two brothers made history.

CHAPTER FOUR

Flying into the Future

Orville and Wilbur Wright conducted special test flights for the army to prove what their aircraft could do.

The Wright brothers continued to experiment and improve their designs. By 1905, they could fly up to 39 minutes at a time and perform exciting **maneuvers** in the air. Three years later, the U.S. military purchased its first airplane from Orville and Wilbur Wright for $25,000. The airplane was big enough to carry both a pilot and a passenger. It had an average speed of about

Today, airplanes are a major part of many countries' militaries.

40 miles (64.4 kilometers) per hour and could travel a lot farther than the Wrights' earlier designs could. Airplanes soon became a major part of militaries around the world, and the Wright brothers began selling planes to a variety of customers.

21st Century Content

Piloting an aircraft was once an incredibly dangerous job. Such famous pilots as Cal Rodgers, Bessie Coleman, and Otto Lilienthal all died in aircraft crashes. Thanks to modern technology, airplane crashes are now very rare. That doesn't mean flying safely is easy, though. All pilots must undergo extensive training before they are allowed to fly on their own. Much of this training involves learning how to safely respond to dangerous situations.

Aircraft technology has gone through many changes since the Wright brothers built their planes. The earliest airplanes were built out of cloth and wood. They were lightweight but not very durable. Inventors soon began experimenting with stronger materials. By the 1930s, most airplanes were built from metal. They were more difficult to damage than wooden planes and could withstand higher speeds.

At the same time, propellers could only provide so much thrust. To build larger, heavier airplanes, engineers began investigating new types of engines. In the 1920s and 1930s, many of them experimented with jet engines. Jets are much more powerful than propellers. In 1930, English engineer Frank Whittle patented his design for a jet engine. The first jet engines were tested seven years later. The first test flight of a jet-powered airplane took place in 1939, using an engine designed by German engineer Hans von Ohain.

Jet engines allow airplanes to fly greater distances at higher speeds, carrying much heavier loads.

Jets opened up a whole new world for airplanes. With more power, engineers were able to design the huge airliners we use to travel around the world today. By the 1960s, jet airliners had replaced ships as the main form of transportation across oceans. More people began using airplanes to travel faster than they ever had before. Today's airplanes continue to become faster and lighter as engineers develop new technology. These airplanes can fly farther and hold more people than older ones could.

Aircraft have come a long way since the experiments of John Damian and Leonardo da Vinci. These early innovators longed to soar through the air as birds do. Today's engineers have not only realized these dreams, but surpassed them. Modern aircraft can fly faster and farther than any bird species can. Thanks to a few brilliant minds who looked to the skies for inspiration, the principals of flight are no longer a mystery. Millions of everyday people take to the skies every day!

CHAPTER FIVE

Famous Flyers

Many pilots have helped to test the limits of aircraft. Here are a few people who have left their marks up in the air.

Calbraith "Cal" Rodgers (1879–1912) was the first man to fly all the way across the United States. Soon after the Wright brothers began selling airplanes to the public, publisher William Randolph Hearst offered a $50,000 prize to the first

Newspaper publisher William Randolph Hearst sponsored a contest for aviators to fly across the United States.

21st Century Content

There are many different jobs for today's aircraft pilots. Some work for commercial airlines. They fly the huge jets people use to travel long distances. Military pilots fly the aircraft used by the Army, the Navy, the Marine Corps, the Air Force, and the Coast Guard. Some pilots find work flying private planes for companies or wealthy individuals. If you are interested in aviation, find out what it takes to become a pilot.

person who could fly across the country in 30 days or less. Rodgers hoped to win. He took off from New York on September 17, 1911, and traveled 4,000 miles (6,437 km) to arrive at the Pacific coast on December 10. Though he was only in the air for about 82 hours, his journey took 84 days. He stopped often for fuel and repairs as he made his way west. He may have missed out on Hearst's prize, but his flight went down in history.

Bessie Coleman (1893–1926) became interested in aviation after attending college and trying her hand as a manicurist and a restaurant manager. She wanted to learn to fly, but racism was an obstacle. Because she was African American, no flight schools in the United States would admit her. Coleman refused to give up. She learned to speak French and moved to France when she was 27 years old to attend flight school there. After graduating, she returned to the United States and began touring the

Bessie Coleman overcame great obstacles in her quest to become a pilot.

country as a stunt pilot. She soon began to draw large crowds and became an inspiration for others who faced discrimination.

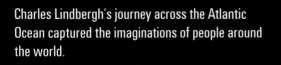

Charles Lindbergh's journey across the Atlantic Ocean captured the imaginations of people around the world.

Charles A. Lindbergh (1902–1974) was the first pilot to make a nonstop solo flight across the Atlantic Ocean. He became interested in aviation during college and went on to work as a stunt pilot and an airmail pilot. In 1926, he was able to convince businessmen in St. Louis, Missouri, to pay for him to fly across the Atlantic. On May 20, 1927, Lindbergh took off from New York in his plane, the *Spirit of St. Louis*. He arrived in Paris, France, the next day. He became a national hero immediately and went on to serve as an adviser to aircraft manufacturers and the U.S. government.

Glossary

ailerons (AY-lur-ahnz) hinged surfaces at the back of an airplane wing used to produce roll

aviation (ay-vee-AY-shuhn) the study, design, construction, maintenance, and operation of aircraft

elevator (EL-uh-vay-tur) a movable horizontal surface used to control the pitch of an aircraft

engineer (en-juh-NEER) a person who is specially trained to design and build machines or large structures

jet (JET) a stream of liquid or gas forced through a small opening with great pressure to produce thrust

maneuvers (muh-NOO-vurz) difficult movements that require planning and skill

momentum (moh-MEN-tum) the tendency of a moving object to continue moving along its original path

pitch (PICH) the degree to which an aircraft's nose is pointing up or down

pressure (PRESH-ur) the force produced by pressing on something

roll (ROL) the movement of an object on an axis parallel to the direction of motion, or side to side

rudder (RUHD-ur) a hinged piece of wood or metal attached to the back of an aircraft and used to control yaw

For More Information

BOOKS

Oxlade, Chris. *Airplanes Inside and Out*. New York: PowerKids Press, 2009.

Solway, Andrew. *Aircraft*. Chicago: Raintree, 2012.

Venezia, Mike. *The Wright Brothers: Inventors Whose Ideas Really Took Flight*.
New York: Children's Press, 2010.

WEB SITES

U.S. Centennial of Flight
www.centennialofflight.gov/index.cfm
Read about the history of flight at this U.S. government site.

Wright Brothers National Memorial
www.nps.gov/wrbr/index.htm
Learn how you can visit the site where Orville and Wilbur Wright tested their
aircraft.

Index

African Americans, 26–27
aircraft
  ailerons, 17
  air pressure, 12
  blimps, 8
  commercial aircraft, 26
  drag, 11
  elevators, 16–17, 18
  engines, 11, 12, 18–19, 22, 24, 26
  gliders, 12–13, 14, 16–17, 18
  hot air balloons, 6–8
  jet engines, 11, 12, 22, 24, 26
  kites, 5, 8, 18
  lift, 12, 13, 14, 16–17
  materials, 22
  military and, 20–21, 26
  passengers, 8, 20, 24
  pilots, 8, 12, 14, 16–17, 18, 19, 20, 22, 25–26, 26–27, 29
  pitch, 17
  propellers, 11, 12, 19, 22
  rolls, 17
  rudders, 17, 18
  runways, 12
  speeds, 12, 20–21, 22, 24
  thrust, 11, 12, 19, 22
  weight, 11, 13, 14, 18–19
  wings, 5, 11, 12, 13, 14, 17, 18
  yaw, 17
  zeppelins, 8

Bernoulli, Daniel, 11
birds
  air pressure, 11–12
  chest muscles, 9
  feathers, 5
  gliding, 11
  lift, 11, 12
  momentum, 11
  observations, 5, 8, 14
  thrust, 11
  wings, 9, 11–12, 14
books, 5, 8, 13, 14

Cayley, George, 12–13, 14
Coleman, Bessie, 22, 26–27

Damian de Falcuis, John, 4–5, 9
da Vinci, Leonardo, 5, 8

Hearst, William Randolph, 25–26
Henson, William, 12

Lilienthal, Otto, 14, 15, 16, 18, 22
Lindbergh, Charles A., 29

Montgolfier, Jacques-Étienne, 6–8
Montgolfier, Joseph-Michel, 6–8

Ohain, Hans von, 22

Rodgers, Calbraith "Cal," 22, 25–26

Taylor, Charlie, 19

Whittle, Frank, 22
Wright, Orville, 15–19, 20, 21
Wright, Wilbur, 15–19, 20, 21

About the Author

Josh Gregory writes and edits books for kids. He lives in Chicago, Illinois.